THE HEART FAMILY BEING KIND IS COOL

Once upon a time, in the big city of Chicago, there lived a close-knit family of 5. There was Daddy Heart, Mama Heart, Tyler Heart (who was 8 years old), Savannah Heart (who was 5 years old), and Chelsea Heart (who was 6 months old). They loved each other very much, and believed in the power of kindness.

As always, on the way to school in the morning, Mama Heart started her daily

affirmations with the children. Affirmations are words that make you feel good

and believe in yourself.

Mama Heart said, "Tyler, you are smart, handsome, and caring. Savannah you are smart, beautiful, and kind. Chelsea, you are smart, beautiful, and joyful!"

Then, Mama Heart screamed, "YOU ARE...."

so Tyler and Savannah screamed.

"THE GREATEST!"

Later on at school that day, Tyler was outside for recess. Tyler was playing with two of his friends when he heard another classmate crying. Tyler told his friends to wait so that he could go see what was wrong with him.

Tyler said, "Hey Jayce, what's wrong?" Jayce replied, "Nothing Tyler." Tyler said, "But

you are crying Jayce. So, what's wrong?" Jayce started to cry harder and said, "David was

bullying me! He always talks about my clothes having holes in them and how my shoes are

always so dirty! He does it to me every day and I am sick of it! I only have what my dad gives

me from my older brother!"

Tyler thought about the affirmations his mom says to him, and how that makes him feel good. Tyler said to Jayce, "Well Jayce, that was very mean of David. He should never talk about you! You are nice, smart, and very helpful! Your clothes don't matter, it's the person inside the clothes that counts!"

Jayce begins to wipe his face and says, "Thank you, Tyler You're right! But, David

always hurts my feelings! He always has something mean to say to me every single day!

My dad says that sticks and stones break your bones, but words will never hurt. He is wrong!

Words DO hurt! I wish I could tell him how I feel, but he always says boys shouldn't cry!"

Tyler was shocked! He never heard his parents say those things. Tyler said. "Well. I can

tell my mom and dad and see what they say. I got nothing. I'm only 8!"

Jayce begins to laugh and the boys run off to play.

Later on at home that night, the Heart Family sat down to eat dinner. Dad asked, "What

was something memorable that happened today?" Savannah said that she won a prize for bingo

at school. Mama Heart said that someone in front of her paid for her coffee. Then, it was Tyler's

turn. Tyler let his family know about what happened with Jayce at school.

Daddy Heart said, "Boys AND Men can absolutely cry. We are human and have

emotions. There are so many boys and men who feel the same way as Jayce. We should not

hold our emotions in because it is not healthy for us. It causes bad things to happen to our

bodies and our minds. Crying can be healing and it releases the stress from your body."

Mama Heart said, "I completely agree!" Also, they shouldn't be speaking bad about Jayce's clothes. Jayce has been through alot and is a nice boy! Kids, do you have any ideas on what we can do as a family to help make Jayce feel better?

Savannah says, "I think we should give Jayce a hug, and maybe get some new clothes for him." Chelsea starts to smile while her sister is talking. Tyler says, "Yes MOM! Can we please buy him some new clothes? You always say we are very blessed and should help others!"

Mama Heart looks at Daddy Heart. He gives her a smile and a head nod. Mama Heart

turns to Tyler and says, "Well, I guess we can! But first, your father and I will need to

make sure that's ok with his dad." The kids start cheering, excitedly.

Mama Heart says, "Ok now, let's all chill. We still have to discuss the bullying. What are we supposed to do when we see someone getting bullied?" Savannah says, "Help them like Tyler did! Good job, brother!" Mama Heart says, "Yes, great job Tyler! What else are we supposed to do if we see it happening?"

Tyler says, "Speak up! Tell the bully to stop and tell an adult that is around what is happening."

Both of his parents smile at him. Dad says, "We taught you right, son!" Tyler then says, "Well Dad,

shouldn't you have a talk with Jayce's dad about telling him not to show how he feels? That

really hurts Jayce's feelings and maybe can be bullying too, right" Dad Heart says, "Well, I guess

I didn't think of that. You're right, son. I will have a talk with Jayce's dad."

That night, Daddy and Mama Heart called Jayce's father. They had a great conversation, and

Jayce's dad agreed to let the Heart Family help them out with clothes for Jayce and his older

brother. Jayce's dad also realized that what he was teaching his sons about emotions was wrong.

He thanked the Heart Family for helping him to see things a different way.

That weekend, Mama Heart took the kids shopping. Jayce was so happy that he was

able to finally express himself to his dad and that he was getting help with his clothes.

Tyler and Jayce agreed to always be friends and have each other's backs! No bullying

allowed!

After spending all day shopping, the Hearts got ready for bed. While Daddy Heart and Mama Heart were tucking Tyler in, they told him that they were very proud of him for helping someone that was being bullied. Tyler said, "You both always tell me that being kind is one of the most important things to be."

Made in the USA
Monee, IL
02 December 2024

72140595R00024